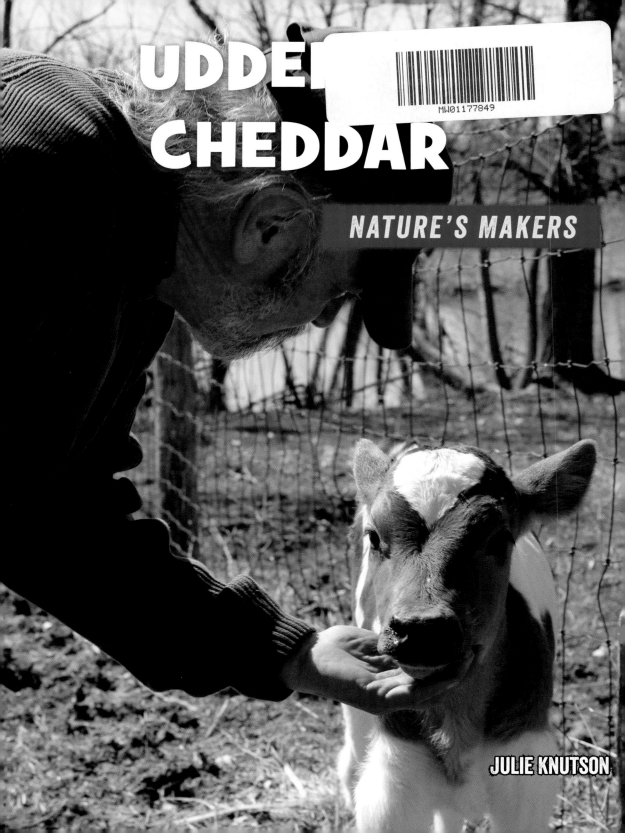

UDDER CHEDDAR

NATURE'S MAKERS

JULIE KNUTSON

Published in the United States of America by Cherry Lake Publishing
Ann Arbor, Michigan
www.cherrylakepublishing.com

Content Advisors: Terry and Denise Woods, owners, Highfield Farm

Photo Credits: © Julie Knutson, cover, 1, 15; © Courtesy of Highfield Farm, 4, 11, 12, 22, 24, 26; © Tyler Rudick, 6; Diane Garcia/Shutterstock.com, 8; © Melody Mellinger/Shutterstock, 16; © Alf Ribeiro/Shutterstock, 18; © gary yim/Shutterstock.com, 29

Library of Congress Cataloging-in-Publication Data
Names: Knutson, Julie, author. | Knutson, Julie. Nature's makers.
Title: Udder to cheddar / by Julie Knutson.
Description: Ann Arbor : Cherry Lake Publishing, 2019. | Series: Nature's makers | Includes bibliographical references and index.
Identifiers: LCCN 2018036612| ISBN 9781534142992 (hardcover) | ISBN 9781534140752 (pdf) | ISBN 9781534139558 (pbk.) | ISBN 9781534141957 (hosted ebook)
Subjects: LCSH: Cheese—Juvenile literature. | Cheesemaking—Juvenile literature. | Farms, Small—Juvenile literature.
Classification: LCC SF271 .K58 2019 | DDC 637/.3—dc23
LC record available at https://lccn.loc.gov/2018036612

Cherry Lake Publishing would like to acknowledge the work of The Partnership for 21st Century Learning. Please visit www.p21.org for more information.

Printed in the United States of America
Corporate Graphics

ABOUT THE AUTHOR

Julie Knutson is a former teacher who writes from her home in northern Illinois. Researching these books involved sampling a range of farm products, from local honey to heirloom grains to...farm-fresh ice cream! She's thankful to all those who accompanied her on these culinary excursions—most notably to the young ones: Theo, Will, Alex, Ruby, and Olivia.

TABLE OF CONTENTS

CHAPTER 1

The Not-So-Big Cheese

State Line Road is one of those unique spots where you can actually hop across state lines. On the south side? Illinois, the "Land of Lincoln." A few steps north? "America's Dairyland," Wisconsin.

Rightly enough, Highfield Farm Creamery sits on the Dairyland side of the street. This tiny **farmstead** is home to a happy herd of 19 cows. It's also home to the cows' caretakers, cheese makers Terry and Denise Woods. Travel with us to meet Terry and Denise, and to learn about what it takes to keep Wisconsin's smallest milking parlor churning.

Highfield Farm Creamery helps Wisconsin earn its nickname of "America's Dairyland."

BEFORE
15,000 YEARS AGO

DOG
Eurasia
15,000 YEARS AGO

SHEEP
Middle East
11,000 YEARS AGO

GOAT
Middle East
10,500 YEARS AGO

PIG
Middle East
10,300 YEARS AGO

HORSE
Central Asia
5,500 YEARS AGO

LLAMA
South America
6,000 YEARS AGO

5,000
YEARS AGO

SILKWORM
East Asia
7,500 YEARS AGO

10,000
YEARS AGO

CAMEL TWO HUMP
Central Asia
4,500 YEARS AGO

CHICKEN
East Asia and Middle East
4,000 YEARS AGO

CAT
Middle East
9,500 YEARS AGO

HONEY BEE
Middle East
10,000 YEARS AGO

COW
Middle East
10,300 YEARS AGO

CAMEL ONE HUMP
Central Asia
3,000 YEARS AGO

A HISTORY OF
DOMESTICATED
ANIMALS

TURKEY
North America
2,000 YEARS AGO

DUCK
East Asia and Middle East
1,000 YEARS AGO

TODAY

HAMSTER
Middle East
LAST 100 YEARS

Dogs are thought to be the first domesticated animal.

Wisconsin is one of America's leading milk and cheese producers. It has more dairy farms than any other state and is home to more than 1.2 million cows. Each year, these cows produce more than 30 billion pounds (13.6 billion kilograms) of milk, making Wisconsin second only to California in milk production.

Wisconsin is also *the* place where that milk gets made into cheese. Whether American or cheddar, mozzarella or feta, Wisconsin makes more cheese than any other place in the United States. It's no wonder that fans of the state's only professional football team, the Green Bay Packers, proudly call themselves Cheeseheads!

Some Wisconsin megafarms house up to 5,000 cows. These massive operations send the cows' milk to manufacturing plants. There, it's processed into cheese. Workers monitor giant vats and operate conveyor belts,

From Wild Ox to Docile Cow

Like goats, sheep, and pigs, cows were first **domesticated** in the Middle East. By examining fossilized DNA evidence, archaeologists have learned that humans began to capture and tame wild oxen into cattle around 10,500 years ago. This would have been a huge challenge for our ancient ancestors. These wild oxen were much larger and not nearly as mild-mannered as the cows we know today!

Farms come in all shapes and sizes. Some megafarms are home to thousands of cows. This contrasts with Highfield Farm, where all 15 to 20 cows are known by name.

making up to 300,000 pounds (136,077 kg) of cheese per week. That's more than 15 million pounds (6.8 million kg) a year!

But not all cheese makers work on this giant scale. Some, like Terry and Denise, prefer to keep it small. The couple makes about 6,000 pounds (2,722 kg) of cheese a year—a fraction of what large manufacturers make in a single *day*. The advantage of their small operation is that they can manage every step of the cheese-making process. They milk their own cows (eight to nine of them at any given time), make their own cheese, and sell that cheese to **consumers** in their own store.

CHAPTER 2

The Road to Cheese Making

How exactly do you get started making cheese by hand?

For Terry and Denise, the path to Highfield Farm was marked by stops and detours. Neither of them grew up on a farm. As kids, neither even had a pet bigger than a guinea pig, let alone cows and chickens!

So how did they end up living on 30 acres (12 hectares) in **rural** southeastern Wisconsin?

Terry spent most of his adult life working in technology. In the early 1980s, he was a pioneer in the computer industry in California. But when Terry and Denise's daughter was born, they got the itch to move back to the Midwest. First, they settled in Illinois, where they lived in the **suburbs**. But the

Terry and Denise have lived in Wisconsin for more than 30 years. In that time, they've renovated and added buildings to their farm to make it a working dairy.

Terry closely monitors all aspects of the cheesemaking process.

couple wanted more land around them. They looked north to Wisconsin.

On a warm February day in 1984, they visited a farm on State Line Road that was for sale. Terry remembers seeing two deer sprint across the property. The family was charmed by the unusually nice temperatures and the idea of antlered neighbors. They had found their new home!

Terry is a man of many hobbies who loves to learn new skills. He's explored the ocean's depths as a scuba diver. He's piloted airplanes and helicopters. And since 2004, he's pursued his passion for cheese.

Terry wanted to learn how to hand-make cheese on a small scale for **commercial production**. The only place he could do this was in Scotland. So, he went to Scotland.

He came back to Wisconsin and learned that all commercial cheese makers in the state need a license. To earn it, he needed to **apprentice** at a cheese plant for 240 hours. He and Denise sent postcards to every cheese plant in the state and got very few responses.

Finally, Terry found the teacher he needed at the University of Wisconsin–Madison. Surprisingly, the school's master cheese maker, Gary Grossen, hadn't worked with students before. Why? Because no one had ever asked him! Terry asked, Gary accepted, and Terry went to Madison. There, he learned how to make dozens of varieties of cheese. He also opened the door for future students who wanted to learn this unique craft from Grossen.

CHAPTER 3

What It Takes

To get the cheese-making operation going, Terry needed milk. He wanted a fresh supply, and he wanted to know its source. What did the cows producing the milk eat? How were they treated? How much time did they spend outdoors? Terry knew that he could only confidently answer those questions if he bought his own cow and milked it himself.

He found Sephora, Highfield's first cow, online. Denise was visiting family in Cleveland when Terry brought Sephora to the farm. She remembers returning home to a new **heifer**. "I would go into the barn and read to her so that she would get used to my voice and not being handled with 150 other cows,"

Calves are usually born between March and July. Here, Terry tends to the first calf of the season, Daffodil.

Jersey cows are a smaller breed of cow known for high milk fat content and smaller environmental hoofprint.

Denise told their local newspaper, the *Walworth County Sunday*.

Other Jersey cows joined the herd. Terry and Denise now had the key **natural resources**—land and cows—needed to make cheese. But they still needed **physical capital**, like **pasteurizers**, to launch a commercial business. They traveled and researched to find the best equipment for **artisanal** operations like theirs. They found a Dutch manufacturer that **specialized** in machines built for small-scale cheese production.

With this in place, the business was up and running.

All types of farms need natural resources, labor, and physical resources.

A World of Resources

Terry and Denise are agricultural **entrepreneurs**. This means they coordinate the resources (or **inputs**) below to make a product (or **output**), in their case, cheese.

Natural Resources—Land and Animals: Natural resources are just what they sound like: materials that come directly from nature. These resources exist without human intervention. Some natural resources, like sun and wind, are **renewable**. Others, like oil and coal, are **nonrenewable**. What natural resources does Highfield Farm need to succeed?

Human Resources—Labor: Human resources are the "people" aspect of any operation. In Terry and Denise's case, it's the knowledge, skills, experience, and abilities that they need to work as cheese makers and business owners. It also includes any occasional help that they need from other employees.

Physical Resources—Capital: Physical resources are the things you need to help operate a business, like machines, computers, and buildings. What physical resources does Highfield Farm need?

Getting to Market

What's an average day on Highfield Farm like? It depends on the time of year!

From May until December, Terry and Denise milk their cows once a day. During these months, milk is in high supply. This is because cows give birth to new calves in the spring and early summer. With the constant flow of milk, Terry and Denise make cheese from their grass-fed cows 2 or 3 days a week. Then, they prepare their products for the weekend, when they sell it at their store and at the farmers' market.

Winters in the Midwest are often snowy and cold. There's no grass on the ground for the cows to eat—they're nibbling

The Jersey cows of Highfield Farm enjoy the outdoors in all seasons.

Denise operates the creamery store on weekends during the summer and fall.
The cheeses that customers sample and buy are made just steps away.

hay and small amounts of corn in the barn. But they still enjoy going outdoors. During this season, the pregnant cows in the herd stop producing milk. With the diminished milk supply, Terry and Denise host cheese tastings, classes, and speaking engagements.

Running a small creamery comes with some challenges. Many consumers want the lowest-priced product, and there are cheaper options than Terry and Denise's handmade cheeses. This is because they are small farmers competing with large **agribusinesses**. The scale of natural, human, and physical resources available to large companies often allows for more product to be made at a lower cost.

Since there are only two of them, Terry and Denise focus on balancing a small, manageable operation that can still be **profitable**. Many people ask if they want to expand, but their goal isn't to grow the business into something larger. Instead, they want to maintain a high-quality, handmade product. At a two-person operation, quality control means limiting growth.

On Saturdays in the summer months, Terry is a fixture at the Fontana Farmers' Market.

Running a two-person **livestock** farm also means that vacations together are rare. After all, someone has to stay with the herd! Denise often gets away to visit family in Ohio, while Terry enjoys long-distance walking trips. Sometimes, these trips even take him back to the place where his cheese-making dream was born—Scotland!

How do Terry and Denise get the word out about Highfield? **Marketing** is a key part of any successful operation. Much of their marketing strategy happens in person and by word of mouth. Loyal customers tell their friends about the business, and soon, they too become regulars at the store.

Terry has also turned another of his hobbies—fixing antique trucks—into a marketing vehicle. Each Saturday during the summer and fall, he arrives at the local farmers' market in an antique Ford Model A. Terry's unique car, branded with Highfield's logo, draws attention to the farm's stand.

News coverage about the farm in local magazines and newspapers also brings customers to the shop and special events. In addition, social media outlets like Facebook and

The Woods family wants Highfield to be a resource for their community.

Instagram allow Terry, Denise, and their herd to connect with admirers all over the world. Each week, Denise posts a new video that highlights the personalities of the cows. In one video, Terry tries to shovel straw but keeps getting nudged by their cow Princess, until he stops and gives her a hug. This sweet moment got more than 4,000 hits and drew comments from viewers as far away as Sweden!

> *"Really small operations like ours can survive, because we aren't beholden to anyone. We have to do our own marketing, we have to milk our own cows, and don't have to worry about a milk source."*
>
> – Terry Woods

Adding acres and cows to Highfield Farm Creamery isn't a priority for Terry and Denise. But opening up their farm to the community is.

Highfield hosts visitors of all ages, from summer campers to nursing home residents. The Woods family wants to show people *where* their food comes from and *how* it gets made.

They also want to show other aspiring cheese makers—
some coming from as far away as Europe and South
America—what can be done on a small scale by two people
and 19 cows.

Agritainment and Agritourism

County fairs. Farm camps. U-pick apple orchards.
Agritainment *and* **agritourism** *are industries with long and growing histories.*

They're also global in popularity. In South Korea, cheese didn't become a part of the food culture until 1958. Now, Imsil Cheese Theme Park offers 32 acres (13 hectares) of dairy-inspired fun in that country.

What can you do at the park? Frolic in the cheese playground, peek at the resident goats, take a cheese-making class, and see the "cheese wheel" building. Of course, you can also sample different types of cheese in one of the park's two restaurants.

Visiting a corn maze in the fall is a type of agritainment.

Read, Research, Write

The Commodities Market...To Sell, or Not to Sell

Unlike many dairy farmers, Terry and Denise operate independently of the **commodities market**. This means they don't sell the milk from Highfield's cows to milk and cheese factories. It also means they don't buy milk from other suppliers.

What's the advantage of working outside of this system of exchange?

Commodities (which include **staples** like milk, grains, and oil) prices are set by the government. These "future market" prices are based on predicted **supply and demand**, and are the payment for product that farmers receive. Sometimes, the formula works in farmers' favor. Other times, it doesn't. Price shifts tend to happen in three-year cycles and are influenced by factors beyond the farm's fields.

What are some of these factors?

When milk demand is predicted to be high but turns out to be low, prices drop and dairy farmers are left with too many cows producing too much milk. Without a market for milk, dairy farmers cannot meet operating costs. As a result, scores of small farms have been forced to close.

The Woods' care for their own small herd. They set prices based on operating costs, level of supply, and what customers are willing to pay. As a result, their business is less exposed to the outside economic stressors that other farms face.

1) What impact would you predict that shifts in milk prices on the commodities market would have on consumers?
2) How might shifting milk prices impact farmers and other businesses in farming communities? How might this impact the broader U.S. and global economies?
3) CONSIDER: Why do you think the government sets commodity prices? What are the pros and cons of price-setting?

GLOSSARY

agribusiness (AG-rih-biz-nis) large-scale, commercial agriculture

agritainment (ag-rih-TAYN-muhnt) farm or agriculture-based entertainment, like hayrides and corn mazes

agritourism (ag-rih-TOOR-iz-uhm) travel and tours centered on visits to farms or ranches

apprentice (uh-PREN-tis) to learn a new skill or trade by working as an assistant to an expert

artisanal (ahr-TIZ-uh-nuhl) made in a traditional way, often by hand

commercial production (kuh-MUR-shuhl pruh-DUK-shuhn) making products to sell to consumers

commodities market (kuh-MAH-dih-teez MAHR-kit) a place where buyers and sellers trade goods in bulk

consumers (kuhn-SOO-murz) people who buy a product

domesticated (duh-MES-tih-kate-id) tamed (an animal) so it can be used by people

entrepreneurs (ahn-truh-pruh-NURZ) people who coordinate resources (natural resources, human capital, physical capital) to create a product and make a profit

farmstead (FAHRM-sted) a farm and the buildings around it

heifer (HEF-ur) female cow that has not had a calf

inputs (IN-puts) factors needed to make a product, such as natural resources, human capital, and physical capital

livestock (LIVE-stahk) farm animals

marketing (MAHR-kit-ing) promoting and advertising a business or service

nonrenewable (nahn-rih-NOO-uh-buhl) natural resources that can run out, such as oil or coal

output (OUT-put) the amount of goods produced using various inputs in a given period of time

pasteurizers (PAS-chur-eye-zurz) machines used to heat milk and kill any harmful microbes

profitable (PRAH-fit-uh-buhl) money making

renewable (rih-NOO-uh-buhl) natural resources that never run out, like the sun and wind

rural (ROOR-uhl) in the country

specialized (SPESH-uh-lized) concentrated on a specific area or need

staples (STAY-puhlz) essential items that people need

suburbs (SUH-burbz) the areas surrounding a city

supply and demand (suh-PLYE AND dih-MAND) the amount of something that is available and the amount that buyers demand it, which is used to determine price

FURTHER READING

Banyard, Antonia, and Paula Ayer. *Eat Up! An Infographic Exploration of Food.* Toronto: Annick Press, 2017.

Carroll, Ricki, and Sarah Carroll. *Say Cheese! A Kid's Guide to Cheese Making with Recipes for Mozzarella, Cream Cheese, Feta, and Other Favorites.* North Adams, MA: Storey Publishing, 2018.

Mickelson, Trina. *Free-Range Farming.* Minneapolis: Lerner Publications, 2016.

Reeves, Diane Lindsey. *Food & Natural Resources: Exploring Career Pathways.* Ann Arbor, MI: Cherry Lake Publishing, 2017.

Vogel, Julia. *Save the Planet: Local Farms and Sustainable Foods.* Ann Arbor, MI: Cherry Lake Publishing, 2010.

INDEX